مُرْشِدُ الْقَارِئ

HA-MEEM PUBLICATIONS
www.hameemstore.com
@hameemstore
orders@hameemstore.com
+1 (416) 879-2545

al-Tanzil Institute of Quranic Sciences
Cape Town, Western Cape,
South Africa
info@al-tanzil.co.za

First Authorized Edition 2024

Al-Tanzil
Institute of Quranic Sciences

Al-Tanzil Institute of Quranic Sciences
Melofin Center, 4 Lawrence Rd,
Athlone, Cape Town, 7764,
South Africa

Tel: (+27) 72 141 7977
E-mail: info@al-tanzil.co.za
Website: www.al-tanzil.co.za

Subject: Grant of Permission to Publish and Copyrights for All Works

Dear HA-MEEM Publications,

Assalamu Alaikum wa Rahmatullahi wa Barakatuh,

I am writing to formally grant Ha-Meem Publications permission to publish, distribute, and manage the copyrights of all my works, including books, articles, and other authored materials. This consent covers all formats, both print and digital.

Please consider this letter as my official authorization for the management and publication of these works, with the expectation that the integrity of the content will be maintained.

Jazakumullahu Khairan for your cooperation.

Sincerely,
Muhammad Saleem Gaibie

S. Gaibie

PREFACE TO SECOND EDITION

I thank my ustādh, Qāri Ayyūb for helping in checking the text of this work and ultimately making the second print an improvement on the first. My gratitude also goes to Sheikh Ismail Londt for his invaluable suggestions. To the students who have studied the book and also contributed in making the third print an improvement on the others.

CONTENTS

Acknowledgements

All my thanks are firstly due to Allah who has granted me innumerable favors and blessings, to which a lifetime of thanks would not do justice.

I also thank Allah for granting me teachers like Moulāna Fārouk Patel and Qāri Ayyūb. I look upon them as a son would his father, thanking Moulāna Fārouk for his unwavering confidence in me and Qāri Ayyūb for being my guide in the past, and present.

I thank my wife, Gafsa for being extremely patient with me and always being a pillar of support through all my endeavors.

My gratitude also goes to my brother and sisters who are always there for me, and the teachers of Dār al-ʿUlūm al-ʿArabiyyah al-Islāmiyyah (DUAI) in Strand for their help, advice and input.

SYSTEM OF TRANSLITERATION

Nr	Arabic	English	Nr	Arabic	English
1	أ	ʾ	17	ظ	ṭḥ
2	ب	b	18	ع	ʿ
3	ت	t	19	غ	gh
4	ث	th	20	ف	f
5	ج	j	21	ق	q
6	ح	ḥ	22	ك	k
7	خ	kh	23	ل	l
8	د	d	24	م	m
9	ذ	dh	25	ن	n
10	ر	r	26	هـ	h
11	ز	z	27	و	w
12	س	s	28	ي	y
13	ش	sh	29	ـَا	ā
14	ص	ṣ	30	ـِي	ī
15	ض	ḍ	31	ـُو	ū
16	ط	ṭ	32	أَيْ	ay
33	أَوْ	ou			

N.B. Arabic words are italicized except in 4 instances:

1- When they possess a current English usage.

2- When they form part of a heading.

3- When they are proper names of people.

4- When they appear in diagrams.

N.B. The sign for [أ] which is [ʾ] will be omitted when the former appears at the beginning of a word.

Foreword

This book is intended for the beginner in *Tajwīd.* The term beginner is used loosely as it still requires him to at least be familiar with the letters of the Arabic alphabet before being able to take maximum benefit from this book.

The book aims at equipping the student with all the basic rules and theory of *Tajwīd* and therefore won't present too many examples as its focus is the theory. Thus without saying, even though the student will get to understand the theory with the aid of this book he requires an able teacher for the practical aspects of *Tajwīd.*

Even though this book is in an English medium since it is aimed at the English speaking person, it will maintain many of the technical terms used in *Tajwīd* which are originally in Arabic. By translating absolutely everything into English the true essence and luster of *Tajwīd* is lost.

This is the first in a series of books. This book is aimed at simplifying the rules of *Tajwīd* for the beginner. Only after understanding and mastering the first book should the student attempt the second. The second book will be written on a higher level; to understand it the pupil should first master the first book. In this manner, by completing all the books in this series, the student would be exposed to all aspects concerning *Tajwīd* being deliberated in the international arena and by experts alike.

Many of the rules written in this book are not necessarily how it is documented by scholars and experts in the field of *Tajwīd.* The reason for this is that the book is aimed at being comprehensive and all-encompassing. If presented exactly as found in other books, many discussions which are to come in the rest of this series on *Tajwīd* will not be properly understood. By studying this book the student doesn't need to refer to another book. This is because other English works in *Tajwīd* have always neglected certain areas in this science. The pupil using these books as aids will get to understand every possible aspect pertaining to the science of *Tajwīd.*

During the various chapters I have placed invaluable notes **(NOTE:)** which are of utmost importance that the student take due care that he learns them. They are of strategic importance for the student in understanding the science and future discussions still to come.

INTRODUCTION TO TAJWĪD

Definition

Tajwīd literally means to do something well. Technically (according to the *qurrā*ʾ), it means to pronounce every letter from its point or place of origin (*makhraj*) together with all its characteristics (*ṣifāt*).

Subject Matter

In *Tajwīd,* we discuss letters of the Arabic alphabet.

Ruling (Ḥukm)

It is *farḍ kifāyah* to learn all the rules of *Tajwīd,* but it is *farḍ ʿayn* to recite the Qurʾān with *Tajwīd.*

Farḍ kifāyah means that if at least one person in the community performs it, the responsibility falls away from the rest of society, but if no-one performs it, the whole community will be answerable for its negligence. *Farḍ ʿayn* means that it is required from every individual.

Benefit

By learning *Tajwīd,* we protect ourselves from making mistakes in the recitation of the Qurʾān.

Mistakes or errors made in the recitation of the Qurʾān are of two types:

1) *Laḥn jaliyy* – a clear error
2) *Laḥn khafiyy* – a hidden error

Laḥn in Arabic means error. *Jaliyy* means clear and *khafiyy* means hidden.

It is called *laḥn jaliyy* (a clear error) because it is clear to everyone listening that an error has been made in the recitation. It is *ḥarām* (prohibited) to recite the Qur'ān with *laḥn jaliyy* on the condition that the *qāri'* (reciter) is aware that he is making *laḥn jaliyy* and that he is making no effort to correct his recitation.

There are basically four ways in which *laḥn jaliyy* can take place:

1) Adding a letter e.g. اَلْحَمْدُوْ لِلهِ
2) Omitting a letter e.g. لَمْ يَلِدْ وَلَمْ يُلَدْ
3) Changing a letter e.g. الهَمْدُ للهِ
4) Changing a vowel (*ḥarakah*) e.g. الحَمْدَ لله

Laḥn khafiyy is made when the *qāri'* falters in the temporary characteristics (صِفَات عَارِضَة) of the letters e.g. *ikhfā', madd* etc.

It is called *laḥn khafiyy* (a hidden error) because the error is hidden or obscure to most people listening to the recitation, and only after studying *Tajwīd* will these errors be recognized by them. It is *makrūh* (disliked) to recite the Qur'ān with *lahn khafiyy* provided that the *qāri'* is aware that he is making *laḥn khafiyy* and that he is making no effort in rectifying his recitation.

TERMS TO KNOW

The Vowels (Ḥarakāt)

The *ḥarakāt* (vowel sounds) in Arabic are indicated by means of a system of strokes above and below the consonantal characters (letters). Every consonant (letter) in Arabic is provided with a vowel sound (*ḥarakah*) or with a sign indicating its absence (*sukūn*).

The vowels are as follows:

- *Fatḥah* (فَتْحَة): a small diagonal stroke above a letter.
- *Kasrah* (كَسْرَة): a small diagonal stroke below a letter.
- *Ḍammah* (ضَمَّة): a small *wāw* above a letter.

The sign indicating the absence of a *ḥarakah* is written directly above a letter e.g. بْ. This is called a *sukūn*.

A letter which has or carries a *ḥarakah* is called *mutaḥarrik*. If it bears a *sukūn* it is called *sākin*.

The Tashdīd

The sign (ّ) is called a *tashdīd* or *shaddah* and the letter which bears a *tashdīd* is called *mushaddad*. The *mushaddad* letter is pronounced twice: the first one always as *sākin* and the second one with a *ḥarakah*, e.g. (مَرَّ) is read as (مَرْرَ) and (دَابَّة) is read as (دَآبْ بَة).

The Tanwīn

Tanwīn means to add a *nūn sākinah* (to the end of nouns). Even though this extra *nūn sākinah* is not written (نْ), it is pronounced. It is indicated by means of a double *fatḥah* (ً), a double *kasrah* (ٍ) or a double *ḍammah* (ٌ) and is pronounced as *'an* (أَنْ), *'in* (إِنْ) and *'un* (أُنْ) respectively e.g. رَحْمَةً is pronounced as رَحْمَتَنْ and مَلَكٌ is pronounced as مَلَكُنْ and صِيَامٍ is pronounced as صِيَامِنْ.

The إسْتِعَاذَة and the بَسْمَلَة

Isti'ādhah means seeking refuge or protection. When mentioning the *isti'ādhah* in *Tajwīd*, we will discuss reciting (أَعُوْذُ بِاللهِ مِنَ الشَّيْطَانِ الرَّجِيْمِ) before starting recitation of the Qur'ān.

Basmalah literally means to recite (بِسْمِ اللهِ الرَّحْمٰنِ الرَّحِيْمِ). The *basmalah* is also recited on commencing the recitation of the Qur'ān and particularly at the beginning of *suwar* (chapters of the Qur'ān).

TERMS TO KNOW:

- فَصْل means to separate.
- وَصْل means to join.
- الأَوَّل means the first.
- الثَّانِي means the second.
- الْكُلُّ / الْجَمِيْع means everything or all.

When discussing the *isti'ādhah* and the *basmalah*, the *qāri'* will find himself in one of three situations if both the *isti'ādhah* and the *basmalah* are being recited:

1. He starts his recitation at the beginning of a *sūrah* (chapter).
2. He starts his recitation in the middle of a *sūrah*.
3. Having already started recitation of the Qur'ān, he is ending a *sūrah* and starting another.

1- In the first situation there are four possible ways of reciting:

1. وَصْلُ الْكُل - to join everything i.e. to join the *isti'ādhah* to the *basmalah,* and the *basmalah* to the beginning of the *sūrah* e.g.

أَعُوْذُ بِاللهِ مِنَ الشَّيْطَانِ الرَّجِيْمِ بِسْمِ اللهِ الرَّحْمٰنِ الرَّحِيْمِ الْحَمْدُ........

2. وَصْلُ الْأَوَّل فَصْلُ الثَّانِي - to join the first (the *isti'ādhah* to the *basmalah*) and separate the second (the *basmalah* from the *sūrah*) e.g.

أَعُوْذُ بِاللهِ مِنَ الشَّيْطَانِ الرَّجِيْمِ بِسْمِ اللهِ الرَّحْمٰنِ الرَّحِيْمْ - اَلْحَمْدُ........

3. فَصْلُ الْكُل - to separate everything i.e. to separate the *isti'ādhah* from the *basmalah,* and to separate the *basmalah* from the beginning of the *sūrah* e.g.

أَعُوْذُ بِاللهِ مِنَ الشَّيْطَانِ الرَّجِيْمْ - بِسْمِ اللهِ الرَّحْمٰنِ الرَّحِيْمْ - اَلْحَمْدُ........

4. فَصْلُ الْأَوَّل وَصْلُ الثَّانِي - to separate the first from the second (the *isti'ādhah* from the *basmalah*) and join the second (the *basmalah* to the beginning of the *sūrah*) e.g.

أَعُوْذُ بِاللهِ مِنَ الشَّيْطَانِ الرَّجِيْمْ - بِسْمِ اللهِ الرَّحْمٰنِ الرَّحِيْمِ الْحَمْدُ

➢ **NOTE:**

All these four ways are permissible.

2 - In the second situation there are also four possible ways of reciting the *isti'ādhah* and the *basmalah* of which two are preferred:

1. فصل الكل - to separate the *isti'ādhah* from the *basmalah,* and to separate the *basmalah* from the middle of the *sūrah* e.g.

أَعُوذُ بِاللهِ مِنَ الشَّيْطَانِ الرَّجِيمِ - بِسْمِ اللهِ الرَّحْمٰنِ الرَّحِيمِ - ذَٰلِكَ الْكِتَابُ

2. وَصْلُ الأَوَّل فَصْلُ الثَّانِي - to join the *isti'ādhah* to the *basmalah,* and to separate the *basmalah* from the middle of the *sūrah* e.g.

أَعُوذُ بِاللهِ مِنَ الشَّيْطَانِ الرَّجِيمِ بِسْمِ اللهِ الرَّحْمٰنِ الرَّحِيمِ - ذَٰلِكَ الْكِتَابُ

➤ **NOTE**:

In this situation وَصْلُ الكُلّ and فَصْلُ الأَوَّل وَصْلُ الثَّانِي is not advised for the beginner.

3 - In the third situation there are also four possible ways of reciting the *isti'ādhah* and the *basmalah* of which three are allowed:

1. فَصْلُ الكُلِّ – to separate everything; the end of the first *sūrah* from the *basmalah* and the *basmalah* from the beginning of the second *sūrah.*

2. وَصْلُ الكُلِّ – to join everything; to join the end of the first *sūrah* to the *basmalah* and join the *basmalah* to the beginning of the second *sūrah.*

3. فَصْلُ الأَوَّل وَصْلُ الثَّانِي – to separate the first *sūrah* from the *basmalah* and join the *basmalah* to the beginning of the second *sūrah.*

➢ **NOTE:**

وَصْلُ ٱلأَوَّل فَصْلُ الثَّانِي will not be allowed as it leaves the impression that the *basmalah* is part of the end of the first *sūrah,* which is not the case.

➢ **NOTE:**

The *basmalah* should not be recited at the beginning of *Sūrah al-Toubah.*

SUMMARY OF THE إِسْتِعَاذَة AND THE بَسْمَلَة

When discussing إِسْتِعَاذَة and بَسْمَلَة the reciter will find himself in one of three conditions

Starting recitation at the beginning of a sūrah

↓

4 ways are allowed

↓

1) fas̱l al-kul
2) fas̱l al-awwal was̱l al-thānī
3) was̱l al-kul
4) was̱l al-awwal fas̱l al-thānī

Starting recitation in the middle of a sūrah

↓

2 ways are preferred for the beginner

↓

1) fas̱l al-kul
2) was̱l al-awwal fas̱l al-thānī

Already started recitation, is ending one sūrah and starting another

↓

3 ways are allowed

↓

1) fas̱l al-kul
2) fas̱l al-awwal was̱l al-thānī
3) was̱l al-kul

NOTE:
Basmalah will not be made when starting from *Sūrah al-Toubah.*

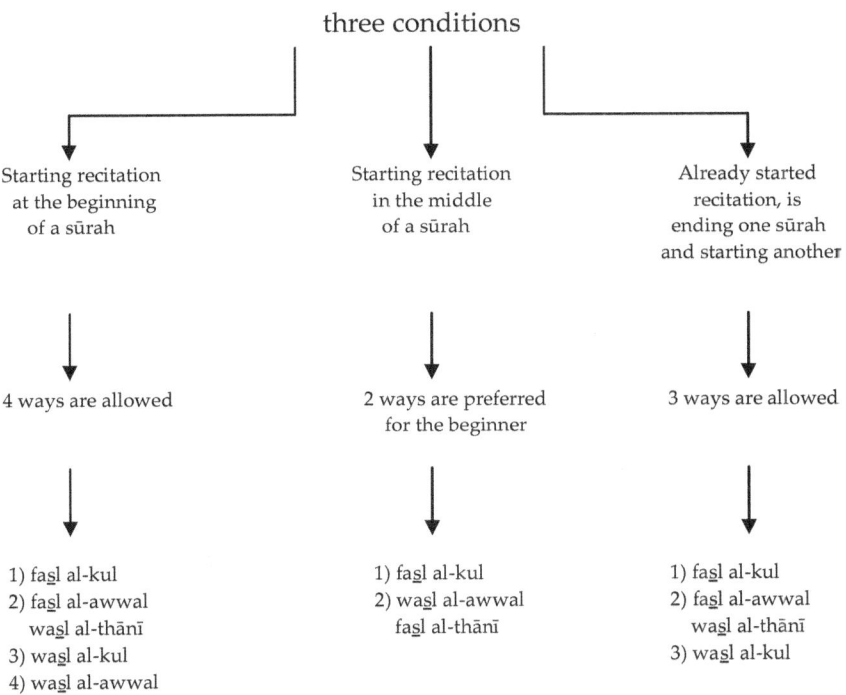

SYNOPSIS OF THE STUDY OF TAJWĪD

Allah commands us in the Qur'ān:

وَرَتِّلِ الْقُرْآنَ تَرْتِيلًا

"*And recite the Qur'ān with tartīl*"

'Ali ﷺ explains that *tartīl* is:

تَجْوِيدُ الْحُرُوفِ وَ مَعْرِفَةُ الْوُقُوفِ

"*Excellence in (the recitation of) the letters and (having) knowledge of waqf*"

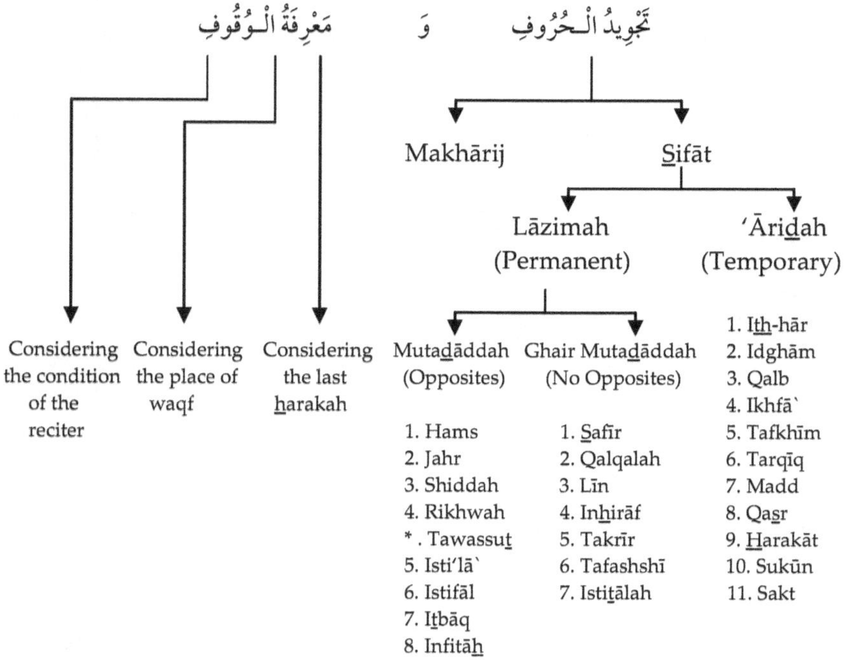

THE MAKHĀRIJ

Makhārij is the plural of *makhraj.* It literally means a place from which something exits. Technically it is an articulation point i.e. that place from which the sounds of the letters are articulated.

Cross section of the organs of speech

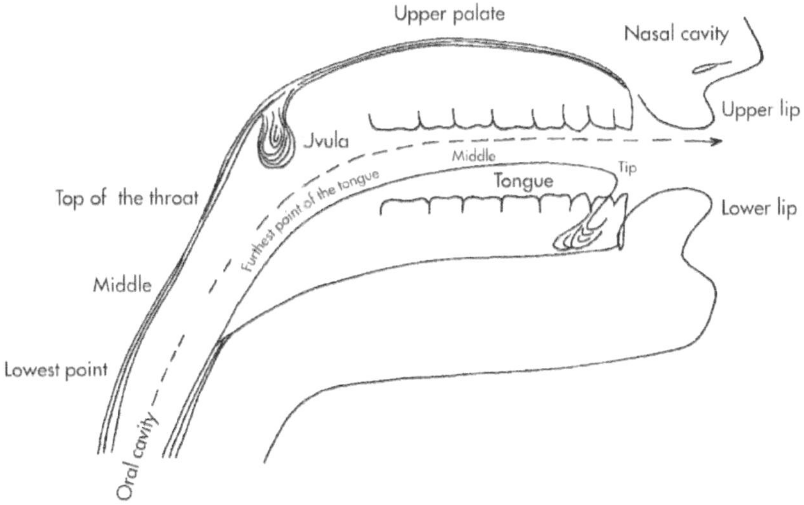

Figure 1: THE ORGANS OF SPEECH

There are 17 *makhārij* (articulation points) according Khalīl Ibn Aḥmad al-Farāhīdī:[1]

1) The empty space in the mouth and throat. The three lengthened letters (*madd* letters) are pronounced from here viz. *wāw sākinah* preceded by a *ḍammah, yā' sākinah* preceded by a *kasrah* and *alif.*

➢ **NOTE:**

The *alif* never takes a *ḥarakah* and is always preceded by a *fatḥah.*

2) The lower throat. This is the part of the throat which is closest to the chest and furthest from the opening of the mouth. The *hamzah* (ء) and *hā'* (ه) are pronounced from here.

3) The middle throat. The *'ayn* (ع) and *ḥā'* (ح) are pronounced from here.

4) The upper throat. This is that part of the throat which is closest to the mouth. The *ghayn* (غ) and the *khā'* (خ) are pronounced from here.

[1] This is also the view held by Ibn al-Jazarī and most contemporary scholars.

Areas of the tongue used for articulation

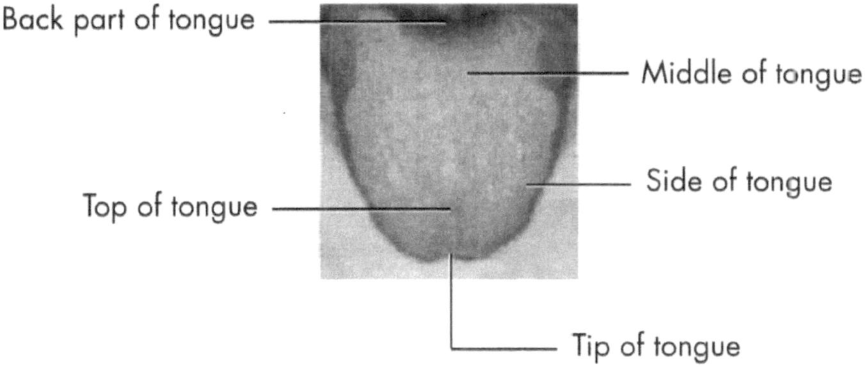

Figure 2: AREAS OF THE TONGUE USED FOR ARTICULATION

5) The extreme back of the tongue, when touching the palate above it (the soft palate). The *qāf* (ق) is pronounced from here.

6) The back of the tongue, not as far the back as the (ق), when touching the palate above it (the hard palate). The *kāf* (ك) is pronounced from here.

➢ **NOTE:**

The back part of the tongue refers to that part of the tongue furthest from the mouth.

7) The centre part of the tongue when touching the palate above it. The *jīm* (ج), *shīn* (ش) and the unlengthened *yā'* (اَلْيَاء غَيْر الْمَدِّيَّة) are pronounced from here.

> **NOTE:**

The *yā' ghayr maddiyyah* - اَلْيَاء غَيْر الْمَدِّيَّة - is either that *yā'* which is *mutaḥarrikah* or which is *sākinah* and preceded by a *fatḥah*. The latter is also called *yā' līn* (ـَيْ).

Teeth and their Names

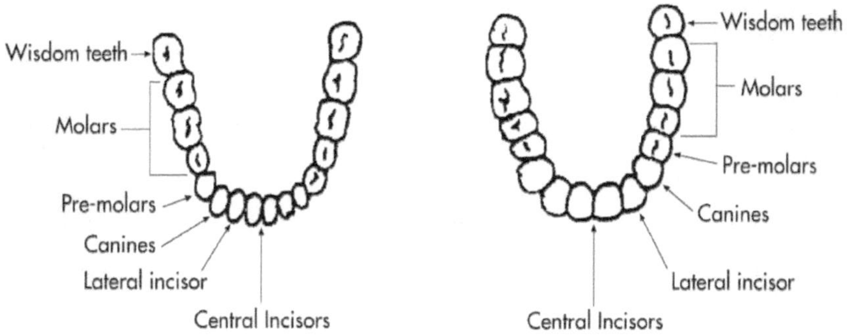

Figure 3: THE TEETH AND THEIR NAMES

8) The side or edge of the tongue when touching the upper molars left or right. It can also be articulated from both sides at once. The *ḍād* (ض) is pronounced from here. The left side is said to be the easiest, followed by the right side. From both sides at the same time is the most difficult.

9) The anterior sides of the tongue (nearest to the mouth) and the tip of the tongue when touching the gums of the teeth extending from one pre-molar to the other. The *lām* (ل) is pronounced from here.

10) The tip of the tongue when touching the gums of the teeth extending from one canine to the other. The *nūn* (ن) is pronounced from here.

11) The tip of the tongue and the top of the tip when touching the gums of the upper central and lateral incisors. The *rā'* (ر) is pronounced from here.

➤ **NOTE:**

Most scholars are of the opinion that the tongue touches the gums of the upper central incisors in the *makhraj* of the *nūn* (ن) and the *rā'* (ر).

12) The tip of the tongue when touching the upper central incisors at the gum line. The *ṭā'* (ط), the *dāl* (د) and the *tā'* (ت) are pronounced from here.

13) The tip of the tongue when touching the edge of the upper central incisors. The *ṭḥā'* (ظ), the *dhāl* (ذ) and the *thā'* (ث) are pronounced from here.

14) Between the tip of the tongue and both central incisors. The *ṣād* (ص), the *sīn* (س) and the *zāy* (ز) are pronounced from here.

➤ **NOTE:**

There is a slight gap between the tongue and the teeth when articulating these letters.

15) The inside of the bottom lip when touching the edge of the upper central incisors. The *fā'* (ف) is pronounced from here.

16) The meeting of the lips. The *wāw ghayr maddiyyah* (اَلْوَاوُ غَيْرِ الْمَدِّيَّة), the *bā'* (ب) and the *mīm* (م) are pronounced from here.

➢ **NOTE:**

The *wāw ghayr maddiyyah* will either be *mutaḥarikah* or *līn*, the same as the *yā' ghayr maddiyyah.*

➢ **NOTE:**

The *wāw* (و) is pronounced with the incomplete meeting of the lips. In articulating the *bā'* (ب) and the *mīm* (م), the lips meet completely.

17) The *khayshūm* (خَيْشُوْم) or nasal cavity. The *ghunnah* or nasal sound comes from here.

THE ṢIFĀT

Ṣifāt is the plural of *ṣifah*. Literally it means qualities or characteristics. Technically, *ṣifāt* are those characteristics which are affixed to the pronunciation of a letter whether intrinsic or circumstantial.

The *ṣifāt* of the letters are of two types:

1. صِفَات لَازِمَة - Intrinsic or permanent *ṣifāt*.

These *ṣifāt* form part of the make-up of the letter i.e. the letter cannot be found without these *ṣifāt*.

2. صِفَات عَارِضَة - Temporary or circumstantial *ṣifāt*. In some conditions these *ṣifāt* are found and in other conditions they are not.

The Ṣifāt Lāzimah

They are divided into two types:

1. مُتَضَادَّة - those *ṣifāt* which have opposites
2. غَيْر مُتَضَادَّة - those *ṣifāt* which have no opposites.

The Mutaḍāddah

Because these *ṣifāt* are *lāzimah*, it is impossible that any letter of the Arabic alphabet be found without these *ṣifāt*, and due to them being opposites, it is also impossible that both opposite *ṣifāt* are found in any one letter! Thus, all letters of the Arabic alphabet must have one of these pairs of *ṣifāt*.

They are:

1. *Hams* (هَمْس) - It literally means a whisper. The breath flows when pronouncing the letters of *hams.* It has 10 letters found in the combination: فَحَثَّهُ شَخْصٌ سَكَتَ.

2. *Jahr* (جَهْر) - It literally means to announce something loudly or publicly. This is the opposite of *hams.* The breath is imprisoned when pronouncing these letters. The letters of *jahr* are all the remaining letters of the Arabic alphabet besides the letters of *hams.*

3. *Shiddah* (شِدَّة) - It literally means strength. The sound is imprisoned when reading these letters. Its letters are found in the combination أَجِدُ قَطٍ بَكَتْ.

4. *Rikhwah/Rakhāwah* (رِخْوَة/ رَخَاوَة) - It literally means softness. This is the opposite of *shiddah.* The sound flows when pronouncing the letters which have *rakhāwah.*

* *Tawassuṭ* (تَوَسُّط) or *bayniyyah* (بَيْنِيَّة) - It literally means in-between. This *ṣifah* is in-between *shiddah* and *rakhāwah.* Its sound does not flow as in *rakhāwah*, nor is it imprisoned as in *shiddah.* Its letters are لِنْ عُمَر.

> **NOTE:**

The letters of *rakhāwah* are all the letters besides the letters of *shiddah* (أجد قط بكت) and *tawassuṭ* (لن عمر).

➤ **NOTE:**

Tawussuṭ is not an independent *ṣifah* because it has a bit of *shiddah* and a bit of *rakhāwah*. For this reason it is not counted as an individual *ṣifah*.

5. *Isti'lā'* (إِسْتِعْلَاء) - It literally means to elevate. The back part of the tongue rises when pronouncing the letters which have this *ṣifah*. It is found in the 7 letters of خُصَّ ضَغْطٍ قِظْ.

➤ **NOTE:**

Due to the back part of the tongue rising, it causes these letters to be pronounced with a full mouth/thick sound (*tafkhīm*).

6. *Istifāl* (إِسْتِفَال) - It literally means to lower. This is the opposite of *isti'lā'*. The back part of the tongue does not rise but instead lays low when pronouncing these letters. It is found in all the letters besides the letters of *isti'lā'*.

➤ **NOTE:**

This action (of the tongue) causes these letters to be pronounced with an empty mouth/thin sound (*tarqīq*).

7. *Iṭbāq* (إِطْبَاق) - It literally means lid or cover. The centre part of the tongue embraces or encompasses the palate. Its letters are *ṣād, ḍād, ṭā'* and *ṭhā'* (ص, ض, ط, and ظ).

➢ **NOTE:**

All the letters of *iṭbāq* have *isti'lā'* in them also.

➢ **NOTE:**

Due to this *ṣifah* these letters are read more full/thick than the *qāf* (ق), the *ghayn* (غ) and the *khā'* (خ) which only have *isti'lā'* in them.

8. *Infitāḥ* (إِنْفِتَاح) - It literally means to open. This is the opposite of *iṭbāq.* The centre of the tongue lies open, not embracing the palate. It is found in all the letters besides the letters of *iṭbāq,* including the *qāf* (ق), the *ghayn* (غ) and the *khā'* (خ).

➢ **NOTE:**

Because the tongue lies open it causes these letters to have a more empty/thin sound in them (*tarqīq*).

➢ **NOTE:**

In *isti'lā', istifāl, iṭbāq* and *infitāḥ,* the action actually takes place in the tongue, but metaphorically we say that it takes place in the letters.

The Ghayr Mutaḍāddah

These *ṣifāt* are also *lāzimah* i.e. it is impossible that a letter having one of these qualities be found without it. However, they do not have any opposites and will only apply to some letters of the Arabic alphabet.

1. *Ṣafīr* (صَفِيْر) - It literally means a whistling sound. It is found in the *ṣād* (ص), the *sīn* (س) and the *zāy* (ز). When these letters are pronounced, there is a whistling sound.

2. *Līn* (لِيْن) - It literally means softness. It is found in the *wāw sākinah* and *yā' sākinah* when they are preceded by a *fatḥah* (-ـَوْ/ـَيْ-). They are pronounced with ease and without much exertion or difficulty.

3. *Inḥirāf* (اِنْحِرَاف) - It literally means inclination. The *makhraj* of these letters incline towards the *makhraj* of another letter. It is found in the *lām* (ل) and the *rā'* (ر).

4. *Takrīr / takrār* (تَكْرِيْر / تَكْرَار) - It literally means to repeat something. It is found in the *rā'* (ر). When it is pronounced, the tongue shudders or shivers (because it repeatedly "knocks" against the palate).

> **NOTE:**

The correct pronunciation of *takrīr* requires us to hide or minimise the *takrīr* and not to exaggerate it.

5. *Tafashshī* (التَّفَشِّي) - It literally means spread out. It is found in the *shīn* (ش). When pronouncing this letter, the breath spreads throughout the mouth.

6. *Qalqalah* (القَلْقَلَة) - It literally means shaking or disturbance. It is found in the letters *qāf, ṭā', bā', jīm, dāl* or the combination قُطْبُ جَدٍّ. When these

letters are pronounced, there is a disturbance in the *makhraj* making it seem as if they are being read with an extra echoing sound.

7. *Istiṭālah* (إِسْتِطَالَة) - It literally means to lengthen. It is found in the *ḍād* (ض). When pronouncing the *ḍād* (ض), the sound is lengthened from the beginning of its *makhraj* till the end i.e. from the beginning of the side of the tongue until its end (until it reaches the *makhraj* of the *lām* - ل).

The Ṣifāt ʻĀriḍah

These characteristics are temporary i.e. sometimes they are found in a letter and sometimes they are not.

They are all 11 in number:

1. *Iṭḥ-hār*
2. *Idghām*
3. *Iqlāb*
4. *Ikhfā'*
5. *Tafkhīm*
6. *Tarqīq*
7. *Madd*
8. *Qaṣr*
9. *Ḥarakāt*
10. *Sukūn*
11. *Sakt*

These 11 *ṣifat* are all menticned in the following two lines of poetry:[2]

إِظْهَارٌ ادْغَامٌ وَ قَلْبٌ وَكَذَا * اِخْفَا وَ تَفْخِيْمٌ وَ رِقٌّ أُخِذَا
وَالْمَدُّ وَالْقَصْرُ مَعَ التَّحَرُّكِي * وَأَيْضًا السُّكُوْنُ وَالسَّكْتُ حُكِيْ

SUMMARY OF ṢIFĀT

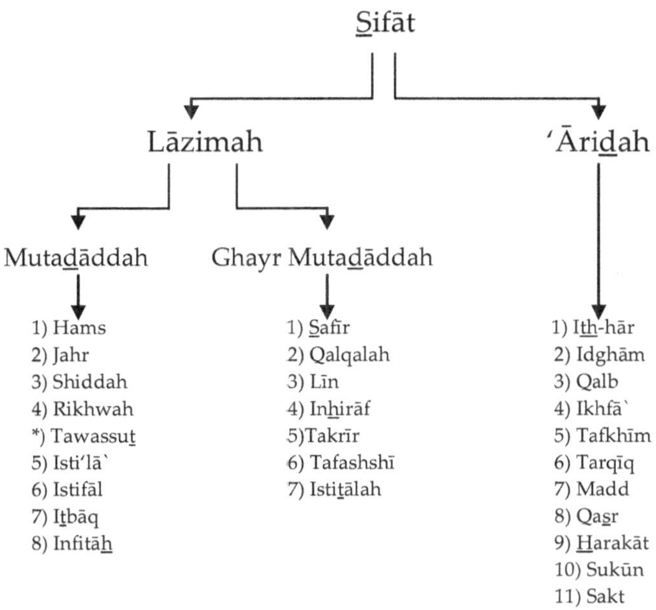

[2] *Al-La'āli' al-Bayān*

TAFKHĪM AND TARQĪQ

Tafkhīm literally means to make something fat or full. In contrast, *tarqīq* means to make something thin.

The letters of the Arabic alphabet can be divided into three categories:

1. Those which are always read with *tafkhīm* or full-mouth.
2. Those which are always read with *tarqīq* or empty-mouth.
3. Those which are sometimes read with *tafkhīm* and sometimes read with *tarqīq*.

Those letters which are always read with tafkhīm.

They are all the letters which have the *ṣifah* of *isti'la'* in them, viz. (خُصَّ ضَغْطٍ قِظْ).

Those letters which are sometimes read with tafkhīm and sometimes with tarqīq.

They are:

1. The *alif* (ا)
2. The *lām* (ل) in the word *Allah*
3. The *rā'* (ر)

Those letters which are always read with tarqīq.

They are all the remaining letters of the alphabet.

The letters which are read with only *tafkhīm* and *tarqīq* can easily be understood. What needs to be learnt however, is the second group of letters: the *alif*, *lām* in the name of *Allah* and the *rā'* - when should they be read with *tafkhīm* and when should they be read with *tarqīq.*

THE ALIF

The *alif* does not have the quality of *tafkhīm* or *tarqīq* but is dependent on the letter before it. If the *alif* (ا) is preceded by a full-mouth letter it will be read with a full mouth and if preceded by an empty-mouth letter it will be read with an empty mouth, e.g. قَالَ , دَارَ.

➢ NOTE

The *tafkhīm* letters (full-mouth letters) are not the letters of *isti'la'* only, but if the *alif* is preceded by a *rā',* then too it will be read with *tafkīm*, e.g. صِرَاطًا , فِرَاقٌ. In these examples, the *rā'* is also a *tafkhīm* letter.

SUMMARY REGARDING THE RULE OF ALIF

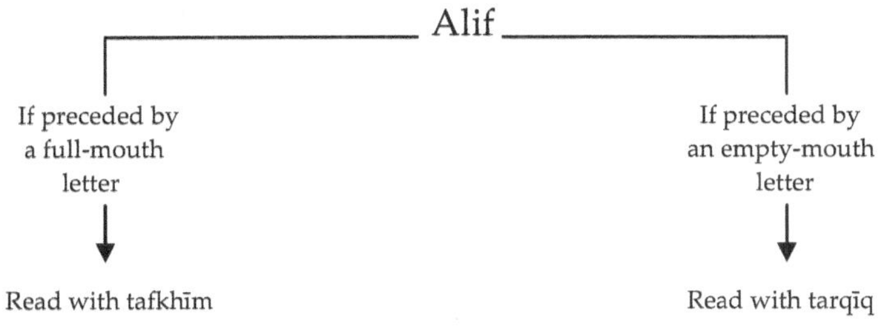
Alif
If preceded by a full-mouth letter
Read with tafkhīm
If preceded by an empty-mouth letter
Read with tarqīq

THE (ل) IN THE NAME (الله)

The (ل) is normally read with *tarqīq*, however, the (ل) which appears in the name (الله) is sometimes read with *tarqīq* and sometimes with *tafkhīm*.

If the (ل) in the name (الله) is preceded by a *fatḥah* or *ḍammah*, it will be read with *tafkhīm*, e.g. اَللّٰهُ, رَسُولُ اللّٰهِ, and if preceded by a *kasrah* it will be read with *tarqīq*, e.g. بِاللّٰهِ.

SUMMARY OF THE LĀM IN الله

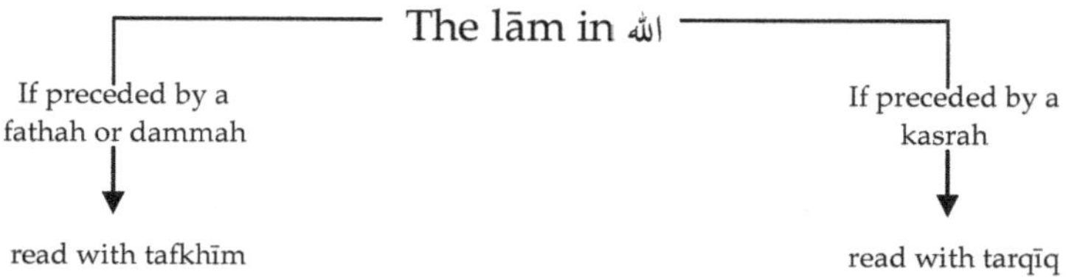
The lām in الله
If preceded by a fathah or dammah
read with tafkhīm
If preceded by a kasrah
read with tarqīq

THE LETTER RĀʾ - ر

The (ر) will be found in one of three conditions:

1. *rāʾ mutaḥarrikah*
2. *rāʾ sākinah* preceded by a *mutaḥarrik*
3. *rāʾ sākinah* preceded by a *sākin* letter which is preceded by a *mutaḥarrik*.

The Rāʾ Mutaḥarrikah

If the (ر) has a *fatḥah* or a *ḍammah*, it will be read with *tafkhīm*, e.g. رَبَّكَ; رُبَمَا and if it has a *kasrah* it will be read with *tarqīq* e.g. رِجَالٌ.

➤ **NOTE**

The *rāʾ mushaddadah* has the same rule like the *rāʾ mutaḥarrikah* i.e. if it has a *fatḥah* or a *ḍammah* it will be read with *tafkhīm*, e.g. سِرًّا,سِرٌّ and if it has a *kasrah*, it will be read with *tarqīq* e.g. ذُرِّيَّةً.

➤ **NOTE**

Rāʾ mumālah (that *rāʾ* in which *imālah* or inclination has taken place) will always be read with *tarqīq*. In *rāʾ mumālah* the *fatḥah* inclines towards the *kasrah* and the *alif* towards the *yāʾ*. There is only one word in the narration of *Ḥafṣ* which is read with *imālah*; مَجْرٖيهَا in *Sūrah Hūd* عليه السلام.

The Rā' Sākinah preceded by a mutaḥarrik

If the *rā' sākinah* is preceded by a *fatḥah* or *ḍammah* it will be read with *tafkhīm*, e.g. يَرْجِعُونَ, يُرْجَعُونَ, اَلْقَمَرْ, اَلتَّكَاثُرْ, and if it is preceded by a *kasrah* it will be read with *tarqīq* e.g. فِرْعَوْنَ, اَلْمَقَابِرْ.

➤ **NOTE**

This rule is applied whether stopping on the *rā'* or continuing (as long as the *rā'* remains *sākin*). If during *waṣl* (continuing) the *rā'* gains a *ḥarakah* then the rules of *rā' mutaḥarrikah* will apply.

There are three exceptions to this rule:

1. If the *kasrah* is temporary e.g. اِرْجِعِي.

Contrary to the rule (that *rā' sākinah* will be pronounced with *tarqīq* if preceded by a *kasrah*), the *rā'* will be read with *tafkhīm* due to the temporary *kasrah*.

➤ **NOTE**

An easy way to check whether the *kasrah* is temporary or not, is to join it to what's before it. If the *kasrah* is not pronounced when joining then it is temporary. If the *kasrah* is read whether joining or starting from it, (in all conditions) then it is permanent.

2. If the *rā' sākinah* is followed by a letter of *isti'lā'* in the same word e.g. مِرْصَادًا, اِرْصَادًا, لَبِالْمِرْصَاد, فِرْقَة and قِرْطَاس. These are the only examples of this in the Qur'ān. Contrary to the rule the *rā'* will be pronounced with *tafkhīm* here.

➢ **NOTE**

We add the condition: "In the same word" to exclude words like فَاصْبِرْ صَبْرًا, قَوْمَكَ أَنْذِرْ and وَلَاتُصَعِّرْخَدَّكَ in which the *rā'* will be read with *tarqīq* because the letter of *isti'lā'* following it is in the next word.

3. The *rā' sākinah* and the *kasrah* must be in one word. If they are in two different words, the *rā'* will be pronounced with *tafkhīm* e.g. اَلَّذِي ارْتَضَى, ارْجِعُونِ رَبِّ, رَبِّ ارْحَمْهُمَا.

➢ **NOTE**

In أَمِ ارْتَابُوا, مَنِ ارْتَضَى, لِمَنِ ارْتَضَى and إِنِ ارْتَبْتُمْ the *kasrah* before the *rā' sākinah* is temporary and it is in a different word to the *rā' sākinah*. Therefore it will be read with *tafkhīm*. These are the only examples of this in the Qur'ān.

➢ **NOTE**

The *rā' mushaddadah* upon which *waqf* (a stop) is made will be read with *tafkhīm* if it is preceded by a *fatḥah* or *ḍammah* e.g. أَيْنَ الْمَفَرُّ, الْمُسْتَقَرُّ and with *tarqīq* if preceded by a *kasrah* e.g. مُسْتَقِرٌّ, مُسْتَمِرٌّ.

The Rā' Sākinah preceded by a sākin letter which is preceded by a mutaḥarrik

If the *mutaḥarrik* has a *fatḥah* or *ḍammah* it will be pronounced with *tafkhīm* e.g. وَالْعَصْرِ, خُسْرٍ and if it has a *kasrah* it will be read with *tarqīq* e.g. ذِكْرٍ.

➢ NOTE

If *rā' sākinah* is preceded by a *yā' sākinah,* it will ALWAYS be read with *tarqīq* eg. خَيْرٌ, خَبِيرٌ. This rule will only apply during *waqf.* During *waṣl* (joining), the *rā'* becomes *mutaḥarrik* and the rules of *rā' mutaḥarrikah* will apply.

Summary of:

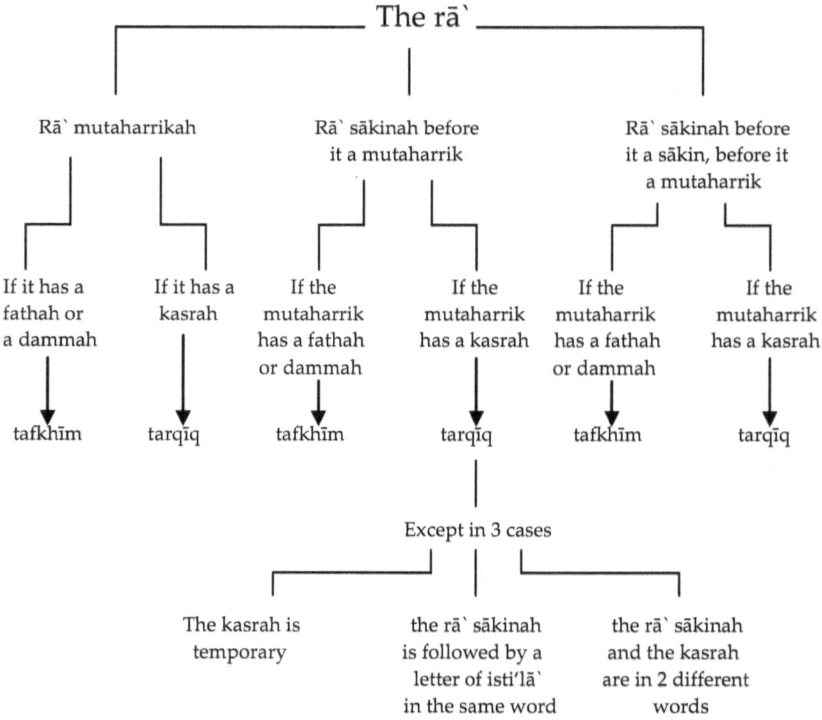

THE RULES CONCERNING THE NŪN (ن) AND THE MĪM (م)

If the (ن) or the (م) are *mushaddadah*, they will be read with *ghunnah* (a nasal sound), e.g. إِنَّ، ثُمَّ.

THE MĪM SĀKINAH

The *mīm sākinah* has three rules:

1. *Ikhfā'* (إِخْفَاء)
2. *Idghām* (إِدْغَام)
3. *Iṭh-hār* (إِظْهَار)

IKHFĀ'

Ikhfā' – It literally means to conceal or hide. If the *mīm sākinah* (مْ) is followed by a *bā'* (ب) then *ikhfā'* will take place; the (م) will be concealed and it will be read with *ghunnah* e.g. تَرْمِيهِمْ بِحِجَارَةٍ، رَبَّهُم بِهِم. This is called *ikhfā' shafawī*.

➤ NOTE

(شَفَة) means lips. (شَفَوِيّ) would refer to a labial pronunciation. It is called (شَفَوِيّ) because the (م) is pronounced from the lips.

IDGHĀM

Idghām – It literally means to assimilate or incorporate. If the *mīm sākinah* (مْ) is followed by another (م) *idghām* will take place i.e. the first *mīm* (م) will be assimilated into the second *mīm* (م) and it will be read with *ghunnah* e.g. كَم مِّن، أَمْ مَّن.

IṬḤ-HĀR

Iṭḥ-hār – It literally means to make clear or apparent. If the *mīm sākinah* (مْ) is followed by any letter besides the *bā'* (ب) (of *ikhfā'*) or the *mīm* (م) (of *idghām*) then *iṭḥ-hār* will take place i.e. the *mīm* (م) will be read clearly without any extra *ghunnah* (nasal pull) in it e.g. اَلْحَمْدُ, أَنْعَمْتَ. This is called *iṭḥ-hār shafawī.*

Summary of: The Rules of Mīm Sākinah

- Ikhfā` → If followed by ب
- Idghām → If followed by م
- Ith-hār → If followed by the remaining letters

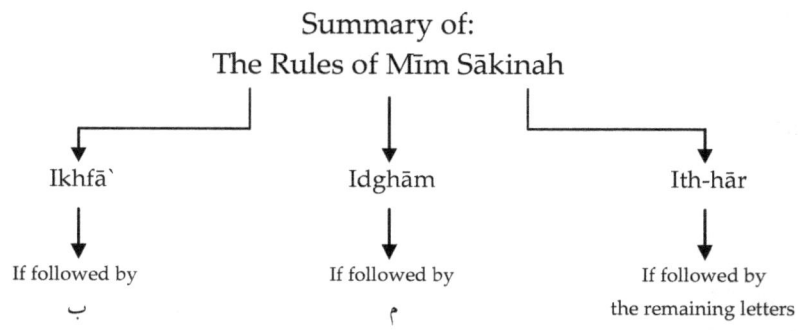

THE NŪN SĀKINAH (نْ) AND TANWĪN (ـً ، ـٍ ، ـٌ)

The rules of the *nūn sākinah* and *tanwīn* are the same because they both have the same pronunciation during *waṣl* (joining) e.g. بْنْ بَ, بِنْ بِ, بُنْ بُ.

The *nūn sākinah* and *tanwīn* have four rules:

1. *Iṭḥ-hār* (إظْهَار)
2. *Idghām* (إدغام)
3. *Iqlāb* (إقْلاَب)
4. *Ikhfā'* (إخْفَاء)

IṬḤ-HĀR

If a *nūn sākinah* or *tanwīn* is followed by any of the letters of the throat (ء, ه, ع, ح, غ, خ), then *iṭḥ-hār* will take place i.e. it will be pronounced clearly without any extra *ghunnah* e.g. أَنْعَمْتَ, كُفُوًا أَحَد.

IDGHĀM

If a *nūn sākinah* or *tanwīn* is followed by any of the letters of (يَرْمَلُوْنَ), then *idghām* will take place.

Idghām is of two types:

1. *Idghām* with *ghunnah*
2. *Idghām* without *ghunnah*

If a *nūn sākinah* or *tanwīn* is followed by a *lām* (ل) or *rā'* (ر), then *idghām* will be made without *ghunnah* e.g. مِنْ رَّبِّ, مِنْ لَّدُنْ. If a *nūn sākinah* or *tanwīn* is followed by any of the letters of (يَنْمُوْ), *idghām* will be made with *ghunnah* e.g. مَنْ يَّقُوْلُ, مِنْ وَّالٍ, مِنْ نِّعْمَةٍ, خَيْرًا يَّرَه, مِنْ مَّاءٍ, خَيْرًا مِّنْهَا.

> **NOTE**

If a *yā'* (ي) or *wāw* (و) appears after the *nūn sākinah* (نْ) in the same word, then instead of *idghām* taking place (as mentioned previously), *iṭḥ-hār* will be made e.g. دُنْيَا, بُنْيَان, قِنْوَان and صِنْوَان. These are the only examples of this in the Qur'ān.

IQLĀB

Iqlāb – It literally means to change.

If a *nūn sākinah* or *tanwīn* is followed by a *bā'* (ب) *iqlāb* will take place i.e. the *nūn sākinah* or *tanwīn* will be changed into a (مْ). As explained previously in the rules of *mīm sākinah* (مْ), if it is followed by a *bā'* (ب), *ikhfā'* will take place and it will be read with *ghunnah* e.g. مِنۢ بَعْدِ, صُمٌّۢ بُكْمٌ.

IKHFĀ'

If a *nūn sākinah* or *tanwīn* is followed by any letter besides (ء, هـ, ع, ح, غ, خ - of *iṭḥ-hār*), (يَرْمَلُوْن - of *idhām*) and (ب - of *iqlāb*) then *ikhfā'* will take place and it will be read with *ghunnah* e.g. أَنْفُسَكُمْ, قَوْمًا ظَلَمُوْا.

The Rules of Nūn Sākinah and Tanwīn

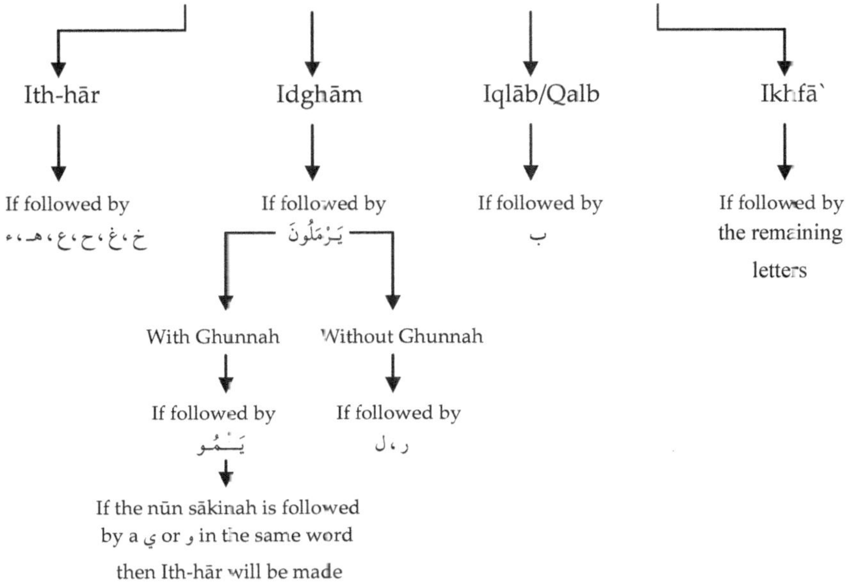

THE MADD

Madd literally means to lengthen or to extend. Technically, it means the lengthening of sound in the letters of *madd* or the letters of *līn.*

The letters of *madd* are three:

1. *Wāw sākinah* preceded by a *ḍammah* (و ـُ)
2. *Yā' sākinah* preceded by a *kasrah* (يْ ـِ)
3. *Alif* (ا ـَ-)

➢ NOTE

The *alif* is always preceded by a *fatḥah.*

The letters of *līn* are two:

1. *Wāw sākinah* preceded by a *fatḥah* (وْ ـَ)
2. *Yā' sākinah* preceded by a *fatḥah* (يْ ـَ)

Initially *madd* is divided into two types:

1. (اَلْمَدُّ الْأَصْلِيّ) – the primary *madd*
2. (اَلْمَدُّ الْفَرْعِيّ) – the secondary *madd*

MADD AṢLĪ

It is that *madd* where after the letter of *madd* there is no *hamzah* (ء) or *sukūn* (ـْ) e.g. نُوْحِيْهَا.

The duration of *madd aṣlī* is one *alif.* One *alif* is referred to as *qaṣr.*

MADD FARʿĪ

It is that *madd* where after the letter of *madd*, there is a *hamzah* or *sukūn.*

The *hamzah* is a cause for two types of *madd*:

1. (اَلْمَدُّ الْمُتَّصِل) – the joined *madd*
2. (اَلْمَدُّ الْمُنْفَصِل) – the separated *madd*

If after the letter of *madd*, the *hamzah* is in the same word together with the letter of *madd,* then it is *madd muttaṣil* e.g. جَاءَ, جِيْءَ, سُوْءُ.

➢ NOTE

It is called the joined *madd* (اَلْمَدُّ الْمُتَّصِل) because the letter of *madd* and the *hamzah* are joined (together) in one word.

If after the letter of *madd,* the *hamzah* forms part of the beginning of the next word, then it is *madd munfaṣil* e.g. بِمَا أُنْزِل, قُوْا أَنْفُسَكُم, فِيْ أَنْفُسِكُم.

➢ NOTE

It is called the separated *madd* (اَلْمَدُّ الْمُنْفَصِل) because the letter of *madd* and the *hamzah* are in separate words.

The duration of *madd muttaṣil* and *madd munfaṣil* is three or four *alifs.* This is also referred to as *tawassuṭ.*

The *sukūn* (ْ) is also a cause for two types of *madd*:

1. (اَلْمَدُّ الْعَارِضُ لِلسُّكُوْن) – the temporary or conditional *madd* (due to *waqf*; stopping).

2. (اَلْمَدّ اللاَّزِم) – the permanent or compulsory *madd.*

If after the letter of *madd* the s*ukūn* is temporary (does not always remain) then it will be *madd ʿāriḍ* e.g. تَعْلَمُوْن, نَسْتَعِيْن, تُكَذِّبَان.

> ➤ **NOTE**

It is called the temporary *madd* because the *sukūn* is temporary.

The duration of *madd ʿāriḍ* is *qaṣr*, *tawassuṭ* or *ṭūl*. *Ṭul* is pulled to the length of five *alifs*. There is no *madd* which is pulled longer than *ṭūl.*

If after the letter of *madd* the *sukūn* is permanent (it remains in all conditions; during *waqf* and *waṣl*) then it will be *madd lāzim* e.g. ءَآلْـئٰنَ, قٓ.

> ➤ **NOTE**

It is called the compulsory *madd* because the *sukūn* is compulsory or permanent.

The duration of *madd lāzim* is *ṭūl* (five *alifs*) only.

TERMS TO KNOW:

(كَلِمِى) – coming from (**كَلِمَة**) meaning word.

(حَرْفِى) – coming from (حَرْف) meaning letter.

(مُخَفَّف) – meaning light, referring to a *sukūn* which is generally light or easy to read.
(مُثَقَّل) – meaning heavy, referring to a *tashdīd*, which is "heavier" in pronunciation than the *sukūn*.

Madd lāzim is initially divided into two types:
1. اَلْمَدّ اللاَّزِم كِلْمِيّ
2. اَلْمَدّ اللاَّزِم حَرْفِيّ

Madd lāzim will be *kilmī* (كِلْمِيّ) if the letter of *madd* and the *sukūn* are found in a word (كَلِمَة).

Madd lazim will be *ḥarfī* (حَرْفِيّ) if the letter of *madd* and the *sukūn* are found in a letter (حَرْف). By letter (حَرْف), the "cut" letters (اَلْحُرُوْف الْمُقَطَّعَات) are specifically referred to e.g. آلٓمٓر, طٰسٓمٓ etc.

The (اَلْحُرُوْف الْمُقَطَّعَات) are only found at the beginning of *suwar* (chapters).

Madd lāzim kilmī and *madd lāzim ḥarfī* are both *mukhaffaf* and *muthaqqal.*

They will be *muthaqqal* (مُثَقَّل) if the *sukūn* is due to *idghām* e.g. وَلاَ الضَّآلِّيْنَ - ضَالْ لِيْنَ, آلٓمٓ - لاَمْ مِيْم.

They will be *mukhaffaf* (مُخَفَّف) if the *sukūn* appears without any *idghām*, e.g. ءآلْآنَ - (أَأَلْـئٰنَ), قٓ - (قَافْ وَالْقُرْآنِ).

MADD LĪN

If after the letter of *līn* there is a temporary *sukūn,* it will be *madd līn ʿāriḍ* e.g. خَوْف, صَيْف. Its duration is *ṭūl, tuwassuṭ* or *qaṣr.*

If after the letter of *līn* the *sukūn* is permanent, it will be *madd līn lāzim* e.g. كٓهٰيٰعٓصٓ, حٰمٓ عٓسٓقٓ (the عَيْنْ in both). These are the only two examples of this *madd* in the Qurʾān.

The duration of *madd līn lāzim* is *tawassuṭ* or *ṭūl. Ṭūl* is preferred.

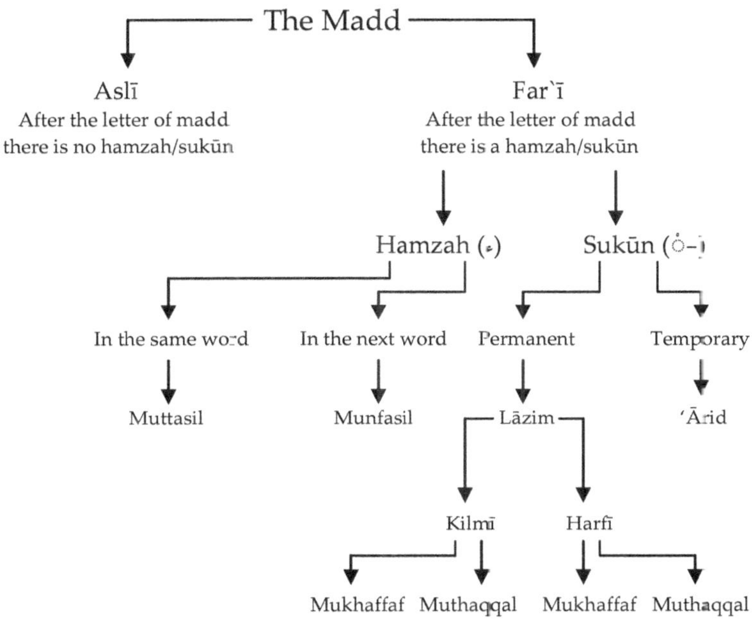
The Madd
Aslī
After the letter of madd
there is no hamzah/sukūn
Far`ī
After the letter of madd
there is a hamzah/sukūn
Hamzah (ء)
Sukūn
In the same word
In the next word
Permanent
Temporary
Muttasil
Munfasil
Lāzim
'Ārid
Kilmī
Harfī
Mukhaffaf
Muthaqqal
Mukhaffaf
Muthaqqal

Madd Līn
'Ārid
Lāzim

WAQF

Previous *qurrā'* would use the terms *waqf*, *qaṭ'* and *sakt* synonymously. With time they, however, came to define the rules more specifically:

Qaṭ' (قَطْع) – It literally means to cut. Technically it means to cut or end the recitation without the intention continuing. *Qaṭ'* is only allowed at the end of *āyāt*.

Waqf (وَقْف) – It literally means to stop. Technically it is to stop at the end of a complete word long enough to renew the breath with the intention of continuing recitation.

Sakt (سَكْت) – It literally means silence. Technically it means to stop the sound whilst reciting without breaking the breath.

When discussing *waqf*, there are three things which are considered:
1. The condition of the *qāri'*.
2. The place where the *qāri'* stops.
3. The *ḥarakah* of the last letter upon which *waqf* is being made.

1. Considering the condition of the *qāri'*, *waqf* is of four types:
1. اَلْوَقْفُ الْاِخْتِبَارِي – the examinatory stop.
This *waqf* is made when being tested (e.g. by a teacher etc.).
This *waqf* is allowed (*jā'iz*) with the condition that the *qāri'* starts his recitation from that particular word again if it doesn't distort the meaning, else he will have to start before the word upon which he made

waqf. If it is at the end of a verse, he should continue his recitation from the next verse.

2. اَلْوَقْفُ الْاِنْتِظَارِي – the adjourning stop.
This *waqf* is made on a particular place solely to complete the various *Qirā'āt*. This *waqf* is also allowed and the *qāri'* will continue reading from that particular word in which the difference of opinion is found. He does not need to repeat what occurs before this word because the object here is to complete all the various *Qirā'āt*.

3. اَلْوَقْفُ الْاِضْطِرَارِي – the forced stop.
This is an involuntary stop made by the *qāri'* which is caused by an unplanned break in his breath due to a cough, sneeze etc. This *waqf* is allowed even though the meaning will be incomplete, but the *qāri'* has to start his recitation from that particular word (on which he stopped) if the meaning allows it, or else he will have to read from before that word.

4. اَلْوَقْفُ الْاِخْتِيَارِي – the voluntary stop.
This is a stop where the *qāri'* chooses to stop at a particular place to renew his breath.

2. Considering the place where the *qāri'* stops, *waqf* is also of four types:
1. اَلْوَقْفُ التَّام – the complete stop.
The *qāri'* makes *waqf* in such a place where the sentence, as well as the meaning, is complete and there is no connection between it and the following verse e.g. وَأُوْلَٰئِكَ هُمُ الْمُفْلِحُونَ (*) إِنَّ الَّذِينَ كَفَرُوا.

> **NOTE**

A connection between two verses can be that they are either connected via their meaning (مَعْنًى) or by their grammar (لَفْظًا). If the verses are connected by their meaning then they do not necessarily have to be connected by their grammar. However, if they are connected by their grammar then they will be connected by their meaning.

2. اَلْوَقْفُ الْكَافِي – the sufficient stop.

The *qārī'* makes *waqf* in such a place where the meaning is connected to the verse following it, but it is not connected grammatically e.g. وَبِالْآخِرَةِ هُمْ يُوقِنُونَ (*) أُوْلَٰئِكَ عَلَىٰ هُدًى مِنْ رَبِّهِمْ.

3. اَلْوَقْفُ الْحَسَن – the sound/good stop.

The *qārī'* stops in such a place where the sentence has a complete meaning, but is connected via its meaning and grammar to what follows e.g. الْحَمْدُ لِلّٰهِ, الْحَمْدُ لِلّٰهِ رَبِّ الْعَالَمِينَ (*).

> **NOTE**

In *waqf tām* and *waqf kāfī,* the *qārī'* will start his recitation after the place of *waqf* whether it's in the middle or the end of a verse. If *waqf ḥasan* is made at the end of a verse, then the *qārī'* will start reciting from the next verse. And if *waqf ḥasan* is made in the middle of a verse, the *qārī'* will have to start from a suitable place before the place of *waqf.*

4. اَلْوَقْفُ الْقَبِيح – the undesirable stop.

The *qārī'* makes a stop in such a place where the sentence is incomplete in that it does not give a sound meaning or gives a corrupted meaning and is connected to what follows in meaning and in grammar e.g. فَاعْلَمْ أَنَّهُ لا إِلٰهَ، يَا أَيُّهَا الَّذِينَ آمَنُوا لا تَقْرَبُوا الصَّلٰوةَ.

> **NOTE**

Waqf qabīḥ is not allowed unless forced to due to expiration of breath, a sneeze or a cough etc.

3. Considering the last *ḥarakah, waqf* is of three types:

1. وَقْف بِالْإِسْكَان – to make *waqf* with *iskān.*

Iskān means to make *sākin.* So وَقْف بِالْإِسْكَان is to stop making the last letter *sākin.* Whether the last letter has a *fatḥah, ḍammah* or *kasrah,* it will be given a *sukūn* during *waqf.*

2. وَقْف بِالرَّوْم – to make *waqf* with *roum.*

This is to make *waqf* on the last letter of the word reading the *ḥarakah* partially. It is only allowed on a *ḍammah* and a *kasrah.*

3. وَقْف بِالْإِشْمَام – to make *waqf* with *ishmām.*

This is to make *waqf* on the last letter of the word by indicating towards the *ḥarakah* with the lips. It is only allowed on a *ḍammah.*

SAKT

Sakt is found in the narration of Ḥafṣ in four places:

1) بَلْ * رَانَ in *Sūrah al-Muṭaffifīn.*

2) مَنْ * رَاقٍ in *Sūrah al-Qiyāmah.*

3) مَرْقَدِنَا * هٰذَا in *Sūrah Yāsīn.*

4) عِوَجًا * قَيِّمًا in *Sūrah al-Kahf.*

Bibliography

Nihāyah al-Qoul al Mufīd by Makkī Naṣr

Al-Nashr fī al-Qirā'āt al-'Ashr by Ibn al-Jazarī

Hidāyah al-Qārī by 'Abd al-Fattāḥ al-Marṣafī

Fawā'ide Makkiyyah by Qāri 'Abd al-Raḥmān al-Makkī

Al-Fawā'id al-Tajwīdiyyah by Qāri Anīs Aḥmad Khān

Salsabīl al-Shāfī by 'Uthmān Murād

Al-La'āli' al-Bayān by Ibrāhīm Samannūdī

OUR PUBLICATIONS

Available at amazon

US

UK

Canada

Beliefs and Practices

Masnoon Duas (Pocket Size)
Arabic with *English*

Daily Wazaaif (Pocket Size)
Arabic with *English*

Al-Hizbul A'zam
(Pocket Size)

Islamic Manners

Etiquettes for Students
آداب المتعلمين

Etiquettes for Teachers
آداب المعلمين

Fazail e Amaal (English)
Virtues of Actions

Fazail e Sadaqaat (English)
Virtues of Spending

Fazail e Ramadan (English)
Virtues of Ramadan

Fazail e Qurbaani (English)
Virtues of Sacrifice

Qurbaani in the Light of the Sunnah

Fasting In The Light Of The Sunnah

The Importance of Performing Salaah with Jamaat in the Musjid

The Adhan

Laws Regarding Trustees of Masaajid & Islamic Organisations

Blessed Life of the Prophet Muhammad ﷺ

Seeratul Mustafa ﷺ (Abridged): English Translation

Muhammad (SAW) - A Mercy unto mankind

Final Days of Rasulullah ﷺ

The Blessed Sunnah of Rasulullah ﷺ - Volumes 1, 2, 3
According to the Hanafi Mazhab

The Blessed Sunnah of Rasulullah ﷺ - Volume 1
According to the Shaafi'ee Mazhab

The Gift of Durood and Salaam
Virtues of Durood and Incidents regarding Love for Rasulullah ﷺ

Hajjatul Wadaa
The Farewell Hajj of Rasulullah ﷺ

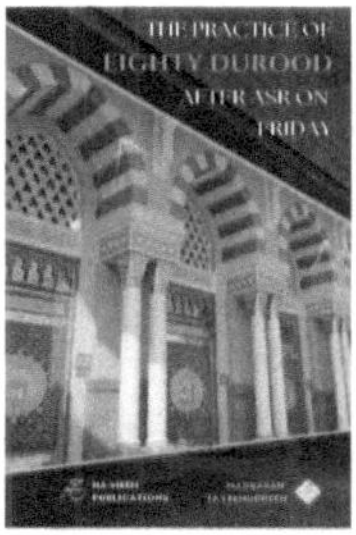

The Practice of Eighty Durood After Asr on Friday

The Selected Forty (Pocket Size)
Collection from Dalāil ul Khairāt

Women and Family

Glimpses of True Beauty from the Lives of Pious Women (Vol. 1)

Glimpses of True Beauty from the Lives of Pious Women (Vol. 2)

Nurturing of Children (Parts 1 to 14)

Happily Ever After
A Muslimah's Guide to a Blissful Marriage

Tuhfatul Banaat
An ideal gift for the young daughters of the Ummah

Tuhfatush Shabaab
A gift for the Youth

Hijaab - In the light of the Qur'aan and Sunnah

Lives of the Pious

Rays of Radiance (Vol. 1)
Inspirational Incidents from the Lives of the Pious

Rays of Radiance (Vol. 2)
Inspirational Incidents from the Lives of the Pious

Scattered Pearls of Moulana Zakariyya Kandhelwi ؒ

Scattered Pearls of Moulana Ashraf Ali Thanwi ؒ

Scattered Pearls of Moulana Muhammad Ilyaas Kandhelwi ؒ

Hadhrat Mufti Mahmood Hasan Gangohi ؒ

Hadhrat Moulana Maseehullah Khan Saahib Sherwaani ؒ

The Life and Mission of Hadhrat Moulana Husain Ahmad Madani ؒ

Hadhrat Moulana Muhammad Qaasim Nanotwi ؒ

Arabic and Other Sciences

From the Treasures of Arabic Morphology - من كنوز الصرف

Miftah ul Qur'an
(Part 1, 2, 3, 4)

The Ten Lessons of Arabic

The Cream of Arabic Imperative Words With Modern Words

Arabic Tutor: Arbi Ka Mu'allim
(Volumes 1, 2, 3, 4)

Solving Tarkeeb
Translation of حَلّ تَرْكِيْب

Qasas Un Nabiyyeen - Part 4
Arabic with *English* Translation

Sharh Miatu Amil
شرح مائة عامل

First Steps to Understanding

First Steps to Understanding Sarf

First Steps to Understanding Arabic ***(Abridged)***

First Steps to Understanding Arabic

First Steps to Understanding Balagah

First Steps to Understanding Logic

First Steps to Understanding Urdu (2nd Edition)

Islamic Reflections and Worldview

In Search of Mount Tur

Spiritual Light VS Material Might

Dhū al-Qarnayn and The Ya'jūj and Ma'jūj

Have You Pondered Over The Message Of Your Creator?

Understanding the Mahdi

How Should A Muslim View Modern Science?

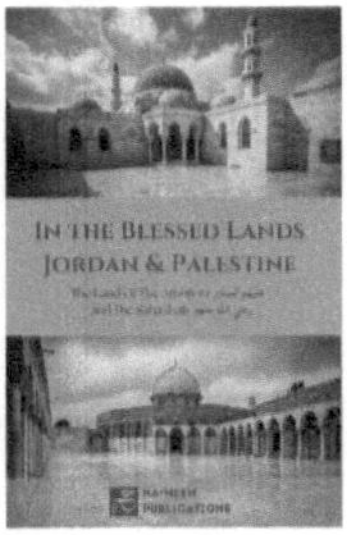

In the Blessed Lands Jordan & Palestine

Spiritual Lessons Derived From SURAH AL-KAHF

The Three Harams

Al-Aqsa - The Past,
The Present, And The Future

Lessons From The Life Of
Salah ad-Din al-Ayyubi

Islamic Theology and Jurisprudence

Taleemul Haq
Five Fundamentals of Islam

Masail Al Qudoori Made Easy
Question Answer Format (English)

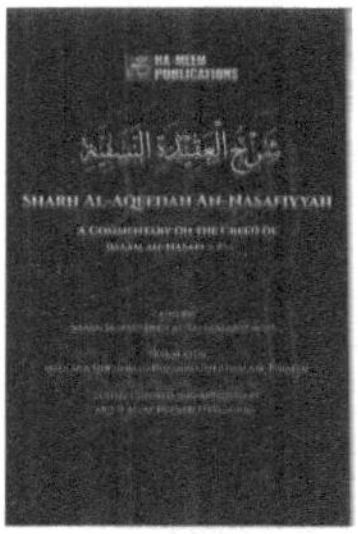

Sharh Al-Aqeedah An-Nasafiyyahs
English Translation

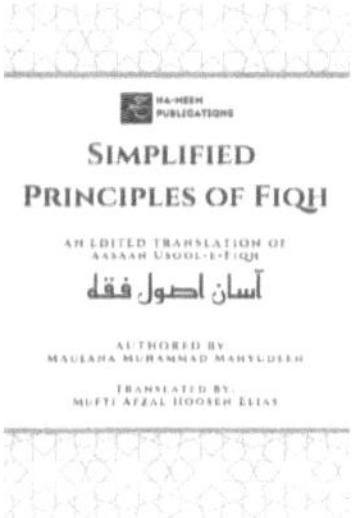

Simplified Principles of Fiqh
Translation of آسان اصول فقه

The Creed of Imam Tahawi
Arabic with *English* & *Farsi* translation

Specialized Texts in Qirā`āt

Fayd al-Mu'in (40 Hadith on the Virtues of the Qur'an)

Commentary on Fayd al-Mu'in

Murshid al Qari - The Guide for Reciters of the Quran

A Commentary of the Tas-hil by Ihab Fikri

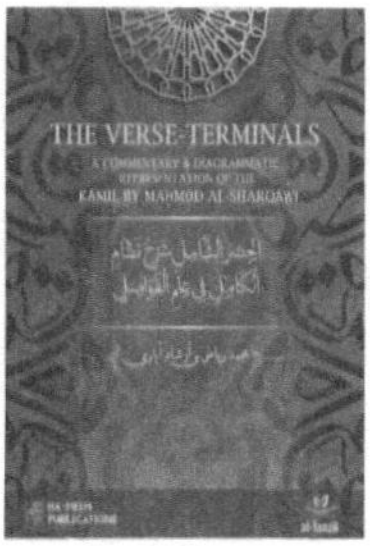

A Commentary of the Kāmil by Maḥmūd al-Sharqāwī

A Simplified Study of the Nāṭhimat al-Zuhr

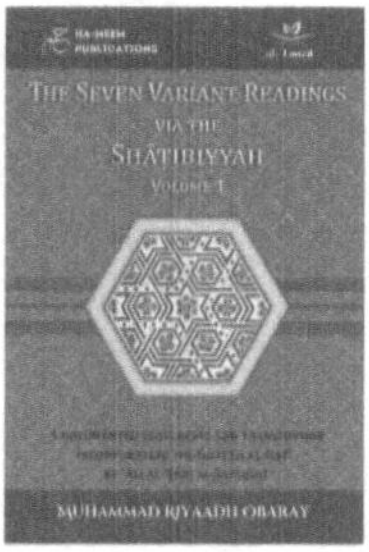

The Seven Variant Readings via the Shatibiyyah - Volume 1

The Gift to the Qurra

Nabr - Lexical Stress in the Quran

Nafaais al-Bayan

al-Tibyan - The Sequence of the Surahs

The Character of Ambassadors of The Quran

A Simplified Study of the Three Variant Readings via the Durrah

The Individual Variants of the Shatibiyyah and Durrah

40 Hadith on Qira'at

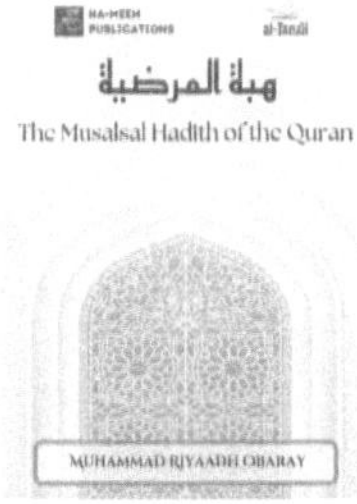

The Musalsal Hadith of the Quran

The Individual Variants of the Shatibiyyah

Irshad Al Qari - Commentary of The Poem Khaqaniyyah

www.ingramcontent.com/pod-product-compliance
Lightning Source LLC
Chambersburg PA
CBHW020338130626
46549CB00003B/1208
* 9 7 8 1 9 9 8 1 1 7 9 9 4 *